PREFACE

The fifty Christmas carols and hymns for upper voices in *Carols for Choirs 4* have been selected from the most widely used choral repertoire and are presented in arrangements for sopranos and altos. Some of the arrangements have been adapted from the familiar mixed-voice versions contained in earlier *Carols for Choirs* volumes; others have been newly written for the present volume. Four original carols for upper voices are included: *A New Year Carol* and *There is no rose* by Benjamin Britten, *I sing of a maiden* by Patrick Hadley, and *Donkey Carol* by John Rutter. The majority of the Christmas hymns included are presented in two versions: for choir only, unaccompanied (suitable for carol singing when a piano or organ is not available), and alternatively for choir and congregation/audience, with accompaniment.

Most of the arrangements are simple, for SSA, though there are a number of more ambitious SSAA settings. 35 of the carols may be sung unaccompanied. Accompaniments supplied are for piano, though some are also suitable for organ, harp, or other instrument(s).

An Order of Service based on the traditional Festival of Nine Lessons and Carols as sung each Christmas Eve at King's College, Cambridge, is given in an appendix.

Many of the arrangements in this book, if sung an octave lower than written, are suitable for male-voice choirs.

OXFORD UNIVERSITY PRESS
MUSIC DEPARTMENT
37 DOVER STREET, LONDON W1X 4AH

INDEX OF TITLES AND FIRST LINES

Where first lines differ from titles the former are shown in italics.

Carols suitable for unaccompanied singing are marked thus*.

Note

Orchestral material for Nos. 6, 9, and 11 is on hire from Oxford University Press.
Orchestral material for No. 23 is on hire from Chappell Music Ltd.
Instrumentation is shown at the foot of the first page of each carol.

1. ANGELS, FROM THE REALMS OF GLORY

Words by
J. MONTGOMERY

Old French tune
arranged by DAVID WILLCOCKS

1. An - gels, from the realms of glo - ry, Wing your flight o'er
2. Shep-herds in the field a - bi - ding, Watch-ing o'er your

all the earth; Ye who sang cre - a - tion's sto - ry
flocks by night, God with man is now re - si - ding;

Now pro - claim Mes - si - ah's birth: Glo -
Yon - der shines the in - fant light: Glo -

- ri - a in ex - cel - sis
- ri - a

Montgomery's original words for the refrain were *Come and worship, Worship Christ the new-born King.*

© Oxford University Press 1980

Printed in Great Britain

Photocopying this copyright material is **ILLEGAL**

De - o,   Glo -
De - o,_____   Glo

De - - - -o!
- - ri - a   in __ ex - cel - sis ____ De - - -o!
- - ri - a __   in   ex - cel - sis   De - - - -o!

3. Sages, leave your contemplations;
    Brighter visions beam afar;
  Seek the great desire of nations;
    Ye have seen his natal star:
      Gloria in excelsis Deo.

4. Saints before the altar bending,
    Watching long in hope and fear,
  Suddenly the Lord, descending,
    In his temple shall appear:
      Gloria in excelsis Deo.

5. Though an infant now we view him,
    He shall fill his Father's throne,
  Gather all the nations to him;
    Every knee shall then bow down:
      Gloria in excelsis Deo.

6

2. ANGELUS AD VIRGINEM

(Gabriel to Mary came)

English translation by
W. A. C. PICKARD-CAMBRIDGE★

14th century
arranged by DAVID WILLCOCKS

★Slightly adapted

A - ve, re - gi - na vir - gi-num; Coe - li ter -rae - que Do - mi -
'All hail, thou queen of vir - gins bright! God, Lord of earth and hea - ven's
A. 'Spi - ri - tus Sanc - ti gra - ti - a Per - fi - ci - et haec om - ni -
'Pow'r from the Ho - ly Ghost_ on high Shall bring to pass this mys - ter-

-num Con - ci - pi - es Et pa - ri - es__ In - ta - cta Sa - lu - tem ho - mi-
height, Thy_ ve - ry Son, Shall soon be born_ in pure - ness, The Sa - viour of__ man-
- a; Ne_ ti - me-as, Sed gau - de - as,_ Se - cu - ra Quod cas - ti - mo - ni-
- y. Then have no fear: Be of good cheer,_Be - liev - ing That still thy chas - ti-

D.S. Verse 2

-num; Tu_ por - ta coe - li fac - ta, Me - de - la cri - mi-num'.
- kind. Thou_ art the gate of hea - ven bright, The sin - ners' heal - er kind.'
- a Ma - ne - bit in_ te pu - ra De - i po - ten - ti - a.'
- ty In_ God's al - might - y keep - ing Shall all un - sull - ied be.'

SEMI-CHORUS

mp

3. Ad haec vir - go no - bi - lis   Re - spon - dens in - quit
3. *Then to him the maid re - plied,*   *With no - ble mien__ su -*
'An - cil - la sum hu - mi - lis   Om - ni - po - ten - tis
'Lo! the hum - ble hand - maid I   *Of God the Lord__ e -*

pp

Ah _____

pp

1st time   *2nd time*

e - i;   De - i.   Ti - bi coe - le - sti nun - ti - o,
-per - nal;   -ter - nal!   *With thee, bright mes - sen - ger__ of heav'n,*

1st time   *2nd time*

Ah _____

Ah _____

Ah _____

Tan - ti se - cre - ti con - sci - o,   Con - sen - ti - ens,   Et
By whom this won - drous news__ is giv'n,   *I__ well a - gree*   *And*

Ah _____   Ah _____

cu - pi - ens__ Vi - de - re Fac - tum quod au - di - o; Pa -
long to see__ Ful - fill - èd Thy gra - cious pro - phe - cy. As__

Ah__

- ra - ta sum__ pa - re - re, De - i con - si - li - o.'
God my Lord__ doth will__ it, So be it un - to me!'

Ah__

ALL VOICES

4. E - ia ma - ter Do - mi - ni, Quae pa - çem red - di - di - sti
4. Hail! thou Mo - ther of the Lord, Who bring'st of gifts__ the ra - rest,

(8va)

PIANO

3. AS WITH GLADNESS MEN OF OLD

(unaccompanied version)

Words by
W. CHATTERTON DIX

Abridged from a chorale, *Treuer Heiland*,
by C. KOCHER (1786–1872)
arranged by DAVID WILLCOCKS

1. As with glad-ness men of old Did the guid-ing star be-hold,
   As with joy they hailed its light, Lead-ing on-ward, beam-ing bright,
   So, most gra-cious God, may we Ev-er-more be led to thee.

2. As with joyful steps they sped,
   To that lowly manger-bed,
   There to bend the knee before
   Him whom heaven and earth adore,
   So may we with willing feet
   Ever seek thy mercy-seat.

3. As they offered gifts most rare
   At that manger rude and bare,
   So may we with holy joy,
   Pure, and free from sin's alloy,
   All our costliest treasures bring,
   Christ, to thee our heavenly King.

4. Holy Jesu, every day
   Keep us in the narrow way;
   And, when earthly things are past,
   Bring our ransomed souls at last
   Where they need no star to guide,
   Where no clouds thy glory hide.

5. In the heav'n-ly coun-try bright Need they no cre-a-ted light;
   Thou its light, its joy, its crown, Thou its sun which goes not down:
   There may we sing
   There for ev-er may we sing Al-le-lu-yas to our King.

3a. AS WITH GLADNESS MEN OF OLD

(congregational version)

Words by
W. CHATTERTON DIX

Abridged from a chorale, *Treuer Heiland*,
by C. KOCHER (1786—1872)
arranged by DAVID WILLCOCKS

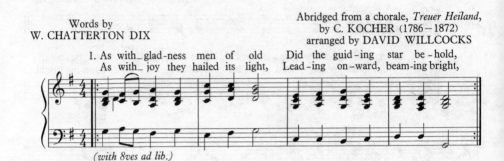

(with 8ves ad lib.)

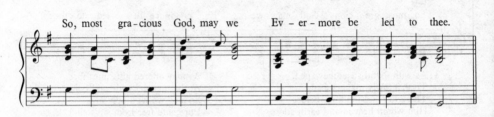

2. As with joyful steps they sped,
   To that lowly manger-bed,
   There to bend the knee before
   Him whom heaven and earth adore,
   So may we with willing feet
   Ever seek thy mercy-seat.

3. As they offered gifts most rare
   At that manger rude and bare,
   So may we with holy joy,
   Pure, and free from sin's alloy,
   All our costliest treasures bring,
   Christ, to thee our heavenly King.

4. Holy Jesu, every day
   Keep us in the narrow way;
   And, when earthly things are past,
   Bring our ransomed souls at last
   Where they need no star to guide,
   Where no clouds thy glory hide.

DESCANT

MELODY

5. In the heav'n-ly coun-try bright Need they no cre – a – ted light;

(with 8ves ad lib.)

Thou its__ light, its joy, its__ crown, Thou__ its sun which__ goes not down:

There for ev – er sing Al-le-lu –yas to__ our King.

There for ev – er may we sing Al – le – lu – yas to our King.

4. AWAY IN A MANGER

Words anon.

W. J. KIRKPATRICK
(1838–1921)
arranged by DAVID WILLCOCKS

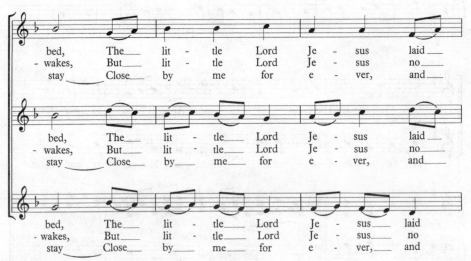

If preferred, the choir may hum or sing *Ah* whilst a soloist sings the words.

16

5. A VIRGIN MOST PURE

English traditional carol
arranged by
JOHN RUTTER

REFRAIN

wrap - pèd us in.
lod - ging at all.

Aye, and there - fore_ be_ mer - ry; Re -

- joice,_ and be you mer - ry; Set_ sor - row_ a - side;_____ Christ

Je - sus_ our_ Sa - viour_ was born_ at this tide.

after v. 2: D.C. for v. 3
after v. 4: straight on for v. 5

VERSES 5 and 6
v. 5: SOLO or SEMI-CHORUS
v. 6: SEMI-CHORUS or SOLO

p 5. The King of all kings to this world be-ing brought, Small
mf 6. Then God sent an an-gel from hea-ven so high, To

SOPRANO

CHOIR   *p* 5. *Lul - la, lul - la, lul - la, lul - la - by.
          mf 6. Al - le - lu - ia, al - le - lu - ia.

ALTO

(Accomp. tacet)

store of fine lin - en to wrap him was sought; And
cer - tain poor shep - herds in fields where they lie, And

Lul - la, lul - la, lul - la - by.
Al - le - lu - ia, al - le - lu - ia.

when she had swad - dled her young son so sweet, With -
bade them no lon - ger in sor - row to stay, Be -

Lul - la, lul - la, lul - la - by.
Al - le - lu - ia, al - le - lu - ia.

* recommended pronunciation *loo-la*

cresc.

-in ___ an ox - man - ger she laid him to sleep.   *Aye, and*
-cause that ___ our ___ Sa - viour was born on this day.

Lul - la,   lul - la,   lul - la - by. ___
Al - le - lu - ia,   al - le - lu - ia.

there - fore ___ be ___ mer - ry; Re - joice, and be you mer - ry; Set

cresc.

Lul - la - by, ___   lul - la, lul - la, ___
Al - le - lu - ia,   al - le - lu - ia, ___

cresc.

(Accomp. doubles voices)

(back to p.19 for v.6)

sor - row ___ a - side; Christ ___ Je - sus ___ our ___ Sa-viour was born at this tide.

lul - la - by. ___   Lul - la,   lul - la, ___   lul - la - by. ___
al - le - lu - ia.   Al - le - lu - ia, ___   al - le - lu - ia.

VERSE 7

ALL VOICES

7. Then_ pre - sent - ly_ af - ter the shep - herds did spy A_ num - ber_ of_ an - gels that stood in the sky; They joy - ful - ly_ talk - èd, and sweet - ly_ did sing, 'To_ God_ be_ all_ glo - ry, our

6. NATIVITY CAROL

Words and music
by JOHN RUTTER

(Man.)

The original version, for mixed voices, is on sale (X169). String parts (suitable for both versions) are on hire.

light__ of star____ He__ who loved _ us so.
babe _ so rare,____ Hearts with his warmth he fills.

light of star____ He__ who loved us so.__
babe so rare,____ Hearts with his warmth he fills.__

- way____ si - lent he lay,____ Born__ to - day,__ your hom - age

Far a - way si - lent he lay, To - day__ your hom - age

Far__ a - way si - lent he lay, To - day__ your hom - age

pay;   For Christ_ is born__ for aye,   Born__ on Christ - mas

pay,   For Christ_ is born__ for aye, __ Born____ on Christ - mas

(Small notes for organ)

2. Cra-dled by mo-ther so fair, Ten-der her lul - la - by; Ov - er her son__ so dear An - gel hosts fill__ the sky.

Day.

Straight on for v.2 S.1
To p.26 for v.4 *p*

S.2
p

A.
Straight on for v.2 (Hum)
To p.26 for v.4

pp (Sw. Salicional 8' + Oct. coupler)

pp

Far__ a - way__ si - lent he lay,__

Far__ a - way__ si - lent he lay,__

(Oct. off)

cresc.   S.1 *mp*

Born — to-day,   your   hom-age   pay;   Christ— is   born— for

S.2

cresc.   A. *mp*

Born — to-day,   your   hom-age   pay;   Christ— is   born— for

mp

dim.   *pp*   Back to p.23 *(from p.25)*
                   for v.3 *pp espress. e dolce*

aye,   Born— on   Christ-mas Day.   4. Love in that   sta-ble was

dim. *pp*   *pp espress. e dolce*

aye,   Born———   on Christ-mas Day.   4. Love in that   sta-ble was

Back to p.23
for v.3   *(from p.25)*

pp   *mp*   *pp* (Salicional 8'
                              Celeste 8')

(Man.)   (Ped.)

ALL VOICES

born,   In-to our   hearts— to   flow;   In-no-cent   dream-ing

28

7. DECK THE HALL

Words traditional

Welsh traditional carol
arranged by
JOHN RUTTER

© Oxford University Press 1980

8. UP! GOOD CHRISTEN FOLK, AND LISTEN

Words by
G. R. WOODWARD

Tune from *Piae Cantiones*, 1582
harmonized by G. R. WOODWARD
adapted by JOHN RUTTER

It is suggested that the first four bars of this setting be repeated at the end.

Words reprinted and harmonies adapted from *The Cowley Carol Book* by permission of A. R. Mowbray & Co.

Come a - dore the new - - - born___ King:
Show - 'ring bless - ings far_____ and___ wide,

Born of mo - ther,___ blest o'er o - ther,___ Ex Ma - ri - a

Vir - gi - ne, In a sta - ble ('tis no fa - ble),

Chri - stus na - tus ho - - di - e.

for Simon Lindley
and the choir of St. Albans School

9. DONKEY CAROL

Words and music by
JOHN RUTTER

A version of this carol for mixed voices is on sale (X254). Orchestral material (suitable for both versions) is on hire.
The instrumentation is 2 Fl, 2 Ob, 2 Cl, Bsn, 2 Hn, Timp and Glock (optional), Hp (optional), and strings.

all with her hea - vy load; _____ Fol - low Jo - seph,
all with his mo - ther mild; _____ Hear the an - gels

lead - ing you on your way Un - til you find a sta - ble,
sing - ing their song on high: 'No-well, no - well, no - well', their

poco rall.   **a tempo**

some - where to rest and stay. _____ Don - key rid - ing
ca - rol - ling fills the sky. _____ Don - key watch - ing

3. Don - key rest - ing all in a man-ger stall,

With the ox - en wor-ship the Lord of all.

Hush, he lies a - sleep on his bed of hay While Ma-ry

lul - la - lay.'

sings so sweet - ly 'Lul - la, lul - la,__ lul - la, lul - la

40   Donkey carol

S. all at the break of day, _____ See, a new light

A. *4. Don - key wak - ing all at the break of day,_____

shin-ing with bright-est ray._____ Long the wea - ry

See, a new light shin - ing with bright-est ray._____

cresc.

jour-ney you soon must start, But you will tra - vel glad - ly;

cresc.

Long the wea - ry jour-ney you soon must start, But you will

*Alternatively, altos may sing *Ah*.

ray._____ No-well, no - well, no-well, no -

ray._____ 5. Don - key skip for

cresc.

- well, no-well, no - well, no-well, no - well, no-well, no - well, no-well, no -

joy as you go your way;_____ Al - le - lu - ia,

- well, no-well, no - well, no - well. Ding-a-dong, ding dong, ding- a-dong, ding dong,

cresc.

Je-sus is born to - day._____ Hark, the bells ring

10. DING DONG! MERRILY ON HIGH

Words by
G. R. WOODWARD

16th-c. French tune
arranged by DAVID WILLCOCKS

i-o pronounced *ee-o*

Words reprinted from *The Cambridge Carol Book* by permission of The Society for Promoting Christian Knowledge.

11. SHEPHERD'S PIPE CAROL

Words and music by
JOHN RUTTER

1. Go-ing through the hills on a night all star-ry
2. 'Tell me, shep-herd boy pi-ping tunes so mer-ri-ly

On the way to Beth - le - hem,__

Far a - way I heard a__
Who will hear your tunes on these

The original version of this carol, for mixed voices, is on sale (X167). Full scores of the mixed-voice version and orchestral material (suitable for both versions) are also on sale. The instrumentation is Picc/Fl, Ob, Bsn, 2 Hn, Hp (optional), and strings.

4. 'Where is this new King, shep-herd boy pi-ping mer-ri-ly,
mp crisply
mp
Ped.
mp
Is he there at Beth - le-hem?'
mf
'I will find him soon by the
mp
mf
Ped.
Ped.
star shi-ning bright - ly In the sky o'er Beth - le - hem.'
(mf)
mf
mp

earth,   and he's ly - ing   cra - dled there at Beth   -   le - hem.'

5. 'May I come with you,   shep-herd

boy   pi - ping mer - ri - ly,   Come with you to Beth   -   le - hem?

12. GOOD KING WENCESLAS

Words by
J. M. NEALE

Tune from *Piae Cantiones*
arranged by DAVID WILLCOCKS

(with 8ves ad lib.)

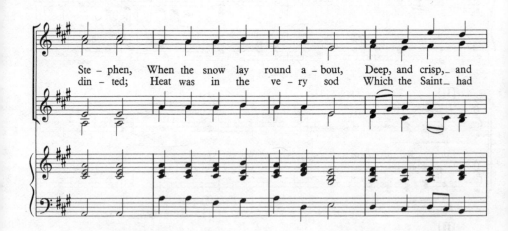

★This carol may be sung unaccompanied.

Congregation / Audience may participate in verses 1, 3 (2nd half), 5, in which case accompaniment should be used.

e – ven: Bright – ly shone the moon that night, Though the frost was
prin – ted. There – fore, Chris – tian men, be sure, Wealth or rank pos –

cru – el, When a poor man came in sight, ___
– sess – ing, Ye who now will bless the poor, ___

(cresc. v. 5)
Ga – th'ring win – ter fu – – – el.
Shall your – selves find bless – – – ing.

Verse 1   Verse 5

(cresc. v. 5)

Verse 1   Verse 5

cresc. v.5

SOLO 1 (ALTO)
SOPRANO
ALTO
f
2. 'Hi – ther, page, and stand by me, If thou know'st it,
mp
Ah
mp
tel – ling, Yon - der pea - sant, who is he? Where and what his
Ah
dwel – ling?'
SOLO 2 (SOPRANO)
mf
'Sire, he lives a good league hence,
pp
Ah
Ah
Ah
pp
Un – der – neath the moun – tain, Right a – gainst the
Ah
Ah
Ah

stron - ger;   Fails my heart, I   know not how;   I   can   go   no

pp

Oo

pp

Oo

SOLO 1 (ALTO)

lon - ger.'   'Mark   my   foot - steps,   good   my   page;

f

mf

Ah

mf

Tread   thou   in   them   bold   —   ly: Thou   shalt   find   the

mf

mp

Ah

Ah

Ah

mp

Ah

D.C. for Verse 5

win - ter's   rage   Freeze   thy   blood   less   cold   —   —   ly.'

13. GOD REST YOU MERRY, GENTLEMEN

(congregational version)

English traditional carol
arranged by DAVID WILLCOCKS

1. God rest you mer - ry, gen - tle-men, Let no-thing you dis - may, For
2. From God our heav'n - ly Fa - ther A bless-ed an - gel came, And

(with 8ves ad lib.)

Je-sus Christ our Sa - viour Was born up-on this day, To save us all from
un - to cer - tain shep - herds Brought ti-dings of the same, How that in Beth-le -

Sa-tan's power When we were gone a - stray: O___ ti - dings of com - fort and
-hem was born The Son of God by name:

joy, com-fort and joy, O___ ti - dings of com - fort and joy.

3. The shepherds at those tidings
Rejoicèd much in mind,
And left their flocks a-feeding,
In tempest, storm and wind,
And went to Bethlehem straightway
This blessèd babe to find:
O tidings of comfort and joy.

4. But when to Bethlehem they came,
Whereat this infant lay,
They found him in a manger,
Where oxen feed on hay;
His mother Mary kneeling,
Unto the Lord did pray:
O tidings of comfort and joy.

God rest you merry, gentlemen

65

13a. GOD REST YOU MERRY, GENTLEMEN

(unaccompanied version)

English traditional carol
arranged by DAVID WILLCOCKS

VERSES 2 & 4

mp 2. From God our heav'n-ly Fa - ther A bless-ed an - gel
p 4. But when to Beth - le - hem they came, Where-at this in - fant

came, And__ un - to cer - tain shep - herds Brought ti - dings of the
lay, They__ found him in a man - ger, Where ox - en feed on

same, How that in Beth - le - hem was born The Son of God by
hay; His mo - ther Ma - ry kneel - ing, Un - to the Lord did

name:__ O__ ti - dings of com - fort and joy, com-fort and
pray:__

D.C. for Verse 3
to next page for Verse 5

joy,__ O__ ti - dings of com - fort and joy.

VERSE 5

Ah _____ Ah _____

5. Now to the Lord sing prais - es, All you with - in this place, And

Ah _____ Ah _____ Ah

Ah _____ Ah _____

with true love and bro - ther-hood Each o - ther now em - brace; Ah This

Ah _____

Ah _____ O ti - dings of

ho - ly tide of Christ - mas All o-thers doth de - face: O ___ ti - dings of

Ah _____ O ___ ti - dings of

com - fort and joy, and joy, O ti - dings of com - fort and joy.

com - fort and joy, com-fort and joy, O ___ ti - dings of com - fort and joy.

com - fort and joy, and joy,_ O ___ ti - dings of_ com - fort and joy.

14. HAIL! BLESSED VIRGIN MARY

Words by
G. R. WOODWARD

Italian carol
arranged by
CHARLES WOOD
adapted by
JOHN RUTTER

1. Hail! Bless-ed Vir-gin Ma - ry! For so when he did meet thee, Spake migh-ty Ga - bri - el, And thus we greet thee. Come weal, come woe, Our hymn shall nev - er va - ry.
2. A - ve, a - ve Ma - ri - a! To glad-den priest and peo - ple, The an - ge-lus shall ring from ev - 'ry stee - ple, To sound his vir - gin birth, Al - le - lu - i - a!
3. Arch - an-gels chant O - san - na, And Ho-ly, Ho - ly, Ho - ly, Be - fore the In - fant born of thee, thou low - ly, Aye - maid - en child of Jo - a - chim and An - na;

Hail! Bless-ed Vir - gin Ma - ry! Hail! Bless-ed Vir - gin Ma - ry!
A - ve, a - ve_Ma - ri - a! A - ve, a - ve_Ma - ri - a!
Arch - an - gels chant O - san - na. Arch - an - gels chant O - san - na.

Hail! Vir - gin_ Ma - ry!
A - ve Ma - ri - a!
An - gels O - san - na.

* If preferred, the first phrase may be sung by 1st sopranos alone.

Words reprinted from *An Italian Carol Book* by permission of The Faith Press Ltd.

15. HARK! THE HERALD ANGELS SING

(congregational version)

Words by C. WESLEY,
T. WHITEFIELD, M. MADAN
and others

MENDELSSOHN
Verse 3 arranged by
DAVID WILLCOCKS

1. Hark! the he - rald an - gels sing___ Glo - ry to the new-born King;
2. Christ, by high - est heav'n a - dored,__ Christ, the e - ver-last - ing Lord,

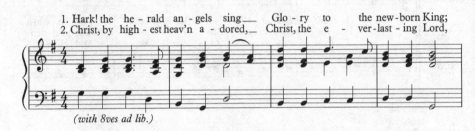

(with 8ves ad lib.)

Peace on earth and mer - cy mild,___ God and sin - -ners re - con-ciled:
Late in time be-hold him come__ Off-spring of a vir - gin's womb:

Joy - ful all ye na - tions rise,___ Join the tri - umph of the skies, __
Veiled in flesh the God-head see,___ Hail th'in-car - nate De - i - ty!___

With th'an - gel - ic host pro - claim, Christ is___ born in Beth - le - hem.
Pleased as man with man to dwell, Je - sus,___ our Em - ma - nu - el.

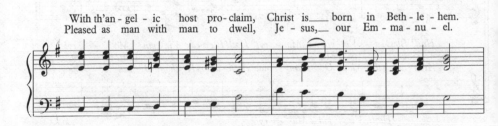

Deity pronounced *Dee-ity*

Melody, and harmony for vv. 1 and 2, adapted by W. H. Cummings (1831–1915) from a chorus by Mendelssohn.

Hark! the he-rald an-gels sing Glo-ry— to the new-born King.

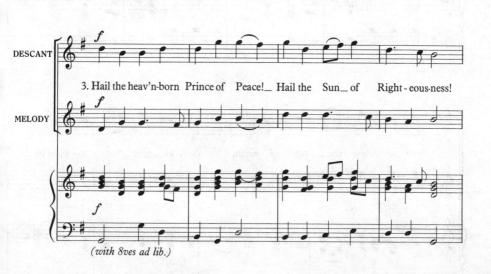

DESCANT

MELODY

3. Hail the heav'n-born Prince of Peace!— Hail the Sun— of Right-eous-ness!

(with 8ves ad lib.)

Light and life to all— he brings,— Ris'n with heal-ing— in his wings;

Mild he lays his glo - ry by,___ Born that man no___ more may___ die,___

Born to raise the___ sons of earth, Born to___give them___ se - cond birth.

ff *cresc.*

Hark! the he - rald an - gels___ sing___ Glo - ry___ to___ the___ new - born King.

15a. HARK! THE HERALD ANGELS SING

(unaccompanied version)

Words by C. WESLEY,
T. WHITEFIELD, M. MADAN
and others

MENDELSSOHN,
adapted by W. H. CUMMINGS
arranged by DAVID WILLCOCKS

1. Hark! the he - rald an - gels sing___ Glo - ry to the new-born King;
2. Christ, by high-est heav'n a - dored,_ Christ, the ev - er - last - ing Lord,
3. Hail the heav'n-born Prince of Peace!_ Hail_ the Sun of Right-eous-ness!

Peace on earth and mer-cy mild,_ God and_ sin - ners re - con - ciled:
Late in time be-hold him come__ Off - spring of__ a vir-gin's womb:
Light and life to all he brings,_ Ris'n with_ heal - ing in his wings;

Joy - ful all ye na - tions rise,_ Join the tri - umph of the skies,_
Veiled in flesh the God-head see,_ Hail th'in - car - nate De - i - ty!__
Mild he lays his glo - ry by, _ Born that man no more may die,_

With th'an - ge - lic host pro - claim, Christ is__ born in Beth - le - hem.
Pleased as man with man to__ dwell, Je - sus,_ our Em - ma - nu - el.
Born to raise the sons of__ earth, Born to__ give them se - cond birth.

Hark! the he - rald an - gels_ sing___ Glo - ry_ to the new - born King.

Hark! the an - gels sing Glo - ry_ to_ the_ new - born King.

Deity pronounced *Dee-ity*

16. A NEW YEAR CAROL

★Words anon.

BENJAMIN BRITTEN

1. Here we bring new wa - ter from the well____ so clear,
2. Sing ___ reign of Fair _ Maid, with ___ gold up - on her toe,
3. Sing ___ reign of Fair _ Maid, with ___ gold up - on her chin,

For to wor - ship God with, this hap - py New Year.
O - pen you the West Door, and turn the Old Year go. } Sing
O - pen you the East Door, and let the New Year in. }

★From *Tom Tiddler's Ground* — Walter de la Mare
Reprinted by permission of Boosey and Hawkes Music Publishers Ltd., London

17. HOW FAR IS IT TO BETHLEHEM?

Words by
FRANCES CHESTERTON

English traditional melody
arranged by DAVID WILLCOCKS

5. Great kings have pre - cious gifts, And we have naught, Lit-tle smiles and

5. Great kings have pre-cious gifts, And we have naught, Lit-tle smiles and

lit - tle tears Are all___ we brought. 6. For all wea - ry chil - dren

6. For all wea - ry chil - dren

tears___ Are all___ we brought. 6. For all wea-ry chil-dren

(6.) Ma - ry must weep. Here, on his bed of straw
(7.) Babes in the byre, Sleep, as they sleep who find

(6.) Ma - ry must weep.___ Here, on___ his bed of straw___
(7.) Babes in the byre,___ Sleep, as___ they sleep who find___

Fine

Sleep, chil - dren, sleep. 7. God in his mo - ther's arms,
Their heart's de - sire.

Sleep,___ chil - dren, sleep. 7. God in his mo - ther's arms,
Their ___ heart's___ de - sire.

D.S.

18. HE SMILES WITHIN HIS CRADLE
(The Cradle)

Words Austrian, 1649
Tr. ROBERT GRAVES

Austrian melody
arranged by DAVID WILLCOCKS

1. He smiles with-in his cra - dle, A babe with face _ so bright _ It beams most like a mir - ror A - gainst a

3. And who _ would rock the cra - dle Where - in this in - fant lies, _ Must rock _ with ea - sy mo - tion And watch with

to next page for Verse 4

blaze_ of   light:_____   This   babe_ so   burn - ing   bright.___
hum - ble   eyes,_____   Like   Ma - ry   pure _ and   wise.___

lul - la,   lul - - la,   lul - la,   lul - la - by.___

- la,   lul - la,   lul - la - by.___

SOLI or SEMI-CHORUS

S.1
S.2

Is Je - sus, Je - sus, is

2. This babe we de - clare_ to you   Is   Je - sus   Christ,_ is

A.

2. This babe_ we now   de - clare_ to you   Is   Je - sus   Christ_ our

cresc.

Haste, haste _ with

Je-sus our Lord;   He brings peace and heart - i - ness: Haste, haste   with

cresc.

Lord;_____   He brings both peace   and   heart - i - ness: Haste, haste   with

D.C. for Verse 3

one_ ac - cord_ To   feast,_ to   feast_with   Christ_our   Lord.___

one_ ac - cord_____   To   feast_with   Christ_ our   Lord.___

19. IL EST NÉ LE DIVIN ENFANT

French traditional carol
arranged by
JOHN RUTTER

(Instrumentalists play from this score.)

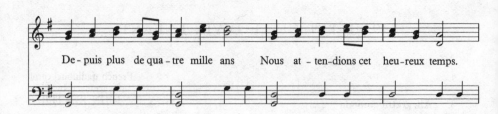

De-puis plus de qua-tre mille ans Nous at - ten-dions cet heu-reux temps.

REFRAIN
f poco leggiero

S.

Il est né le di - vin en -fant, Jou-ez haut-bois, ré-son-nez mu- set - tes;

A.

f poco leggiero

f

Last time: to CODA

Il est né le di - vin en -fant, Chan-tons tous son a - vè - ne-ment.

Last time: to CODA

1st and 3rd times

S.

2. Ah! qu'il est beau, qu'il est char-mant,   Ah! que ses grâ - ces___ sont par - fai - tes!
4. O Jé – sus, roi___ tout puis-sant,   Si pe-tit en - fant___ que vous ê - tes;

A.

mp
(Accompt. tacet)

REFRAIN D.S.

Ah! qu'il est beau, qu'il est char-mant,   Qu'il est___ doux, ce di-vin en - fant!___
O Jé – sus, roi___ tout puis - sant,   Rég - nez___ sur nous en - tiè - re ___ ment.___

2nd time

mf

S.1
Ah   Ah

S.2
A.
3. Une é - ta-ble est son lo - ge-ment,   Un peu de paille est___ sa cou-chet - te;
(Accompt. tacet)

REFRAIN D.S.

poco rit.

Ah   Ah

Une é - ta-ble est son lo - ge-ment,   Pour un Dieu quel a - bais-se - ment!___

CODA

rit.

mf   *dim.*   *p*

20. IN DULCI JUBILO

(4-part version)

Words tr.
R. L. de PEARSALL

German traditional carol
arranged by
R. L. de PEARSALL
adapted by JOHN RUTTER

VERSES 1 and 2

SOPRANO

1. In dul - ci ju - bi - lo_____ Let us our
2. O Je - su par - vu - le!_____ I yearn for

ALTO

hom - age shew;_____ Our heart's joy_____ re - clin - -
thee al - way!_____ Hear me, I_____ be - seech_____

- - eth In prae - se - pi - o_____ And
_____ thee, O Puer op - ti - me!_____ My

like a bright_____ star shin - eth Ma - tris in
prayer_____ let_____ it reach_____ thee, O Prin - ceps

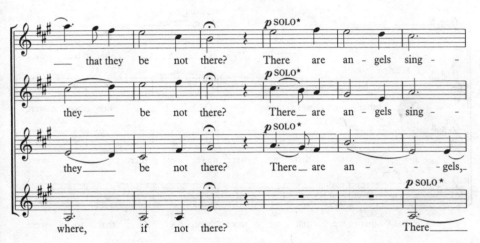

* or a few voices

90

20a. IN DULCI JUBILO

(3-part version)

Words tr.
R. L. de PEARSALL

German traditional carol
arranged by
JOHN RUTTER (vv. 1, 2, 4)
R. L. de PEARSALL (v. 3)

© Oxford University Press 1980

gre - mi - o.____ Al - pha es et
glo - ri - ae!____ Tra - he me post
cu - ri - a:____ O that we were

O,____ Al - pha es et O.
te,____ tra - he me post te!
there,____ O____ that we were there!

VERSE 3 (may be sung by solo voices)

SOPRANO 1   3. O Pa - tris ca - ri - tas,

SOPRANO 2   3. O Pa - tris ca - ri - tas,

ALTO   3. O Pa - tris ca - ri - tas,____ O Na - ti

O Na - ti le - ni - tas!____

O Na - ti le - ni - tas! Deep - ly

le - ni - tas!____ Deep - ly were we

21. I SAW THREE SHIPS

English traditional carol
arranged by DAVID WILLCOCKS

22. IT CAME UPON THE MIDNIGHT CLEAR

English traditional melody
adapted by ARTHUR SULLIVAN
arranged by DAVID WILLCOCKS

Words by
E. H. SEARS

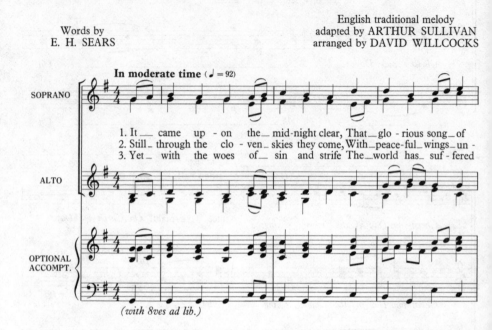

1. It __ came up - on the __ mid-night clear, That __ glo - rious song __ of
2. Still __ through the clo - ven __ skies they come, With __ peace-ful __ wings __ un -
3. Yet __ with the woes of __ sin and strife The __ world has suf - fered

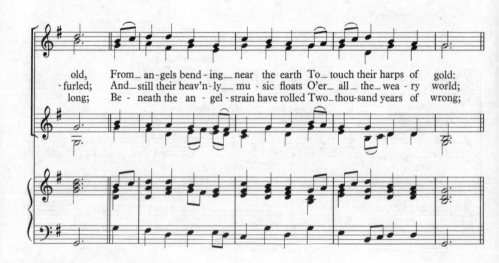

old, From __ an-gels bend - ing __ near the earth To __ touch their harps of gold:
- furled; And __ still their heav'n - ly __ mu - sic floats O'er __ all __ the __ wea - ry world;
long; Be - neath the an - gel - strain have rolled Two __ thou-sand years of wrong;

'Peace on the earth, good - will to men, From heav'n's all - gra - cious King!'
A - bove its sad and low - ly plains They bend on ho - v'ring wing;
And man, at war with man, hears not The love - song which they bring:

The world in so - lemn still - ness lay To hear the an - gels sing.
And ev - er o'er its Ba - bel sounds The bless - ed an - gels sing.
O hush the noise, ye men of strife, And hear the an - gels sing!

By pro - phets fore - told,

4. For lo! the days are has - t'ning on, By pro - phet - bards fore - told,
4. For lo! the days are has - t'ning on, By pro - phet - bards fore - told,

4. For lo! the days are has - t'ning on, By pro - phet - bards fore - told,

23. I SING OF A MAIDEN

Words traditional

PATRICK HADLEY

Orchestral material (2 Fl, Ob, 2 Cl, 2 Hn, Strings) is on hire from Chappell Music Ltd.

24. THE CHERRY TREE CAROL

English traditional carol
arranged by DAVID WILLCOCKS

SOPRANO

mf 1. Jo-seph was an old — man, And — an — old — man was he, —
p 3. O then be-spoke Ma - ry, With — words both meek and mild, —
mp 5. Then bowed down the high-est tree Un - to — our — La - dy's hand; —
p 7. Then Ma - ry plucked a cher - ry, As — red — as — a - ny blood, Then

ALTO 1
ALTO 2

vv. 1 & 7   *(vv. 3 & 5)*

p   *vv. 3 & 5:* Ah

vv. 1 & 7: Ah   Ah —

v.7: rall. e dim.   *Fine*

When he — mar - ried — Ma - ry In the land of Ga - li - lee.
'Pluck me — one cher-ry, Jo - seph; For — that I am with child.'
'See,' Ma-ry cried 'see, — Jo - seph, I have cher-ries at com - mand.'
Ma - ry — went she — home-wards All — with her hea - vy load. —

A.1

mp 2. And as — they were walk - ing Through an — or - chard so good, —
mf 4. 'Go to the tree then, Ma - ry, And — it — shall bow to thee; And
mf 6. 'O eat your — cher-ries, Ma - ry, O — eat — your cher-ries now; O

S.
A.2

p Ah

p   Ah

Ah   Ah —

D.C. for vv. 3, 5, 7

Where were cher-ries and ber - ries As — red as a - ny blood. —
you shall ga - ther cher - ries By — one, by two, by three.' —
eat your cher - ries, Ma - ry, That — grow up - on the bough.' —

Ah

© Oxford University Press 1980

25. KING JESUS HATH A GARDEN

Words tr.
G. R. WOODWARD

Dutch carol
arranged by
JOHN RUTTER

1. King Jesus hath a garden full of divers flow'rs, Where I go culling posies gay, all times and hours. There naught is heard but Paradise bird, Harp, dulcimer, lute, With cymbal, trump and tymbal,

3. The bonny Damask-rose is known as Patience: The blithe and thrifty Marygold, Obedience. There naught is heard but bird, Harp,

6. Ah! Jesu Lord, my heal and weal, my bliss complete, Make thou my heart thy garden-plot, fair, trim and neat. That I may hear this musick clear: Harp,

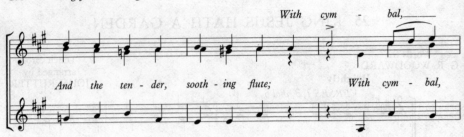

With cym - bal,

And the ten - der, sooth - ing flute; With cym - bal,

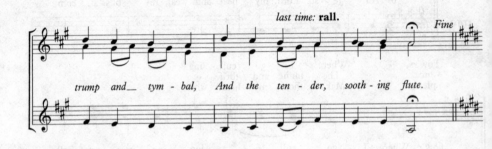

last time: **rall.**

Fine

trump and tym - bal, And the ten - der, sooth - ing flute.

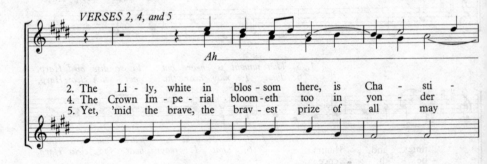

VERSES 2, 4, and 5

Ah

2. The Li - ly, white in blos - som there, is Cha - sti -
4. The Crown Im - pe - rial bloom - eth too in yon - der
5. Yet, 'mid the brave, the brav - est prize of all may

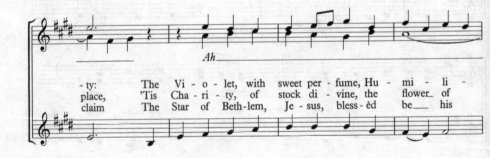

Ah

- ty: The Vi - o - let, with sweet per - fume, Hu - mi - li -
place, 'Tis Cha - ri - ty, of stock di - vine, the flower of
claim The Star of Beth-lem, Je - sus, bless - èd be his

*Small notes are alternatives.

26. ROCKING

Tr. PERCY DEARMER

Czech carol
arranged by DAVID WILLCOCKS

If preferred, the accompanying voices may hum or sing *Ah*.

Words and melody from *The Oxford Book of Carols* by permission

27. COVENTRY CAROL

Words from the Pageant of
the Shearmen and Tailors (15th c.)

adapted from the
original version (1591)
by JOHN RUTTER

*Accompaniment may be played on a keyboard instrument or sung by a semi-chorus.

VERSES 1, 2, and 3

(SOLO or FULL)

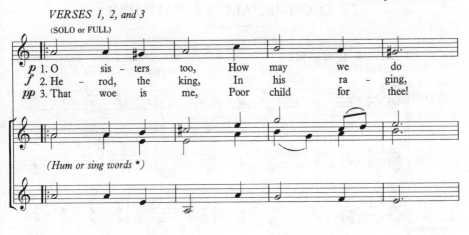

p 1. O   sis - ters   too,   How   may   we   do
f 2. He - rod,   the   king,   In   his   ra - ging,
pp 3. That   woe   is   me,   Poor   child   for   thee!

(Hum or sing words ★)

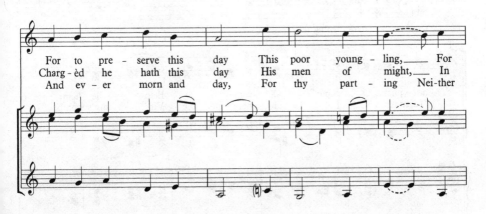

For   to   pre - serve   this   day   This   poor   young - ling,____ For
Charg - èd   he   hath   this   day   His   men   of   might,____ In
And   ev - er   morn   and   day,   For   thy   part - ing   Nei-ther

after v.3: REFRAIN D.C.

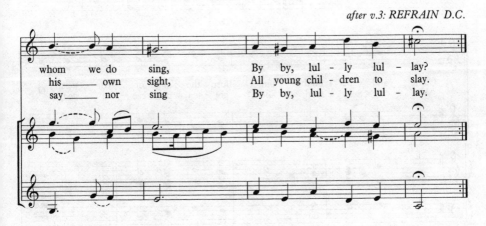

whom   we   do   sing,   By   by,   lul - ly   lul - lay?
his____ own   sight,   All   young   chil - dren   to   slay.
say____ nor   sing   By   by,   lul - ly   lul - lay.

★Hum here if words were sung in refrain, and vice versa.

28. O COME, ALL YE FAITHFUL

(Adeste Fideles)

Tr. F. OAKELEY, W. T. BROOKE
and others

Composer unknown (probably 18th c.)
arranged by DAVID WILLCOCKS

1. O come, all ye faith-ful, Joy-ful and tri-um-phant, O come ye, O come ye to Beth-le-hem; Come and be-hold him Born the King of An-gels: O
2. God of God, Light of Light, Lo! he ab-hors not the Vir-gin's womb; Ve-ry God, Be-got-ten, not cre-a-ted:

(with 8ves ad lib.)

(loco)

This hymn may be sung unaccompanied.

(with 8ves ad lib.)

3. See how the shepherds,
   Summoned to his cradle,
   Leaving their flocks, draw nigh with lowly fear;
   We too will thither
   Bend our joyful footsteps:
       O come, etc.

4. Lo! star-led chieftains,
   Magi, Christ adoring,
   Offer him incense, gold and myrrh;
   We to the Christ Child
   Bring our hearts' oblations:
       O come, etc.

5. Child, for us sinners
   Poor and in the manger,
   Fain we embrace thee, with awe and love;
   Who would not love thee,
   Loving us so dearly?
       O come, etc.

to next page for v.6

(with 8ves ad lib.)

let us a - dore___ him,   Christ___ the Lord!

let us a - dore___ him, ___ Christ the Lord!

come, let us a - dore___ him, ___ Christ___ the Lord!

come, let us a - dore___ him, ___ Christ the Lord!

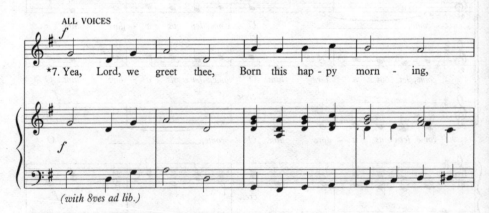

ALL VOICES

*7. Yea, Lord, we greet thee, Born this hap - py morn - ing,

(with 8ves ad lib.)

*Omit this verse if no accompaniment is available.

29. O LITTLE TOWN OF BETHLEHEM

Words by
PHILLIPS BROOKS

English traditional tune
arranged by DAVID WILLCOCKS

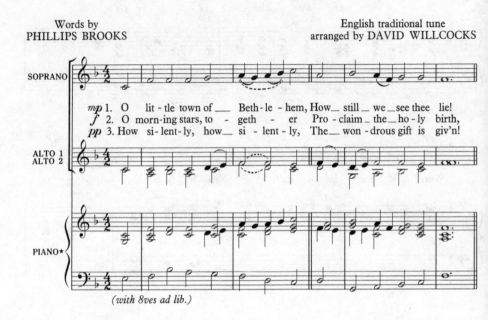

mp 1. O lit - tle town of ___ Beth - le – hem, How__ still _ we _ see thee lie!
f 2. O morn-ing stars, to - geth - er Pro - claim _ the _ ho - ly birth,
pp 3. How si - lent-ly, how__ si - lent - ly, The__ won -drous gift is giv'n!

(with 8ves ad lib.)

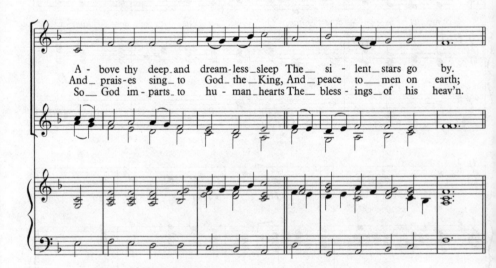

A - bove thy deep and dream-less_sleep The _ si - lent_stars go by.
And_ prais-es sing_ to God_ the _King, And_ peace to__ men on earth;
So__ God im - parts_ to hu - man_hearts The bless - ings_ of his heav'n.

Melody collected and adapted by R. Vaughan Williams and used by permission

The harmonies used in the first four bars are based on those by R.V.W. by permission.

★One or more verses may be sung unaccompanied.

Yet__ in   thy dark__ streets__ shi - neth   The__ ev - er - last - ing   light;__
For __Christ   is born__ of __ Ma - ry;   And, gath-er'd__ all__ a - bove,__
No__ ear   may hear__ his__ com - ing;   But__ in   this__world__ of   sin,__

The__ hopes and fears of   all__ the__years__ Are__ met__ in__thee to - night.
While__ mor -tals sleep, the   an - gels__ keep__ Their watch of __won-d'ring love.
Where__ meek souls will re - ceive__him,__ still __The__ dear__ Christ en - ters in.

S.1
S.2
O   ho - ly__ Child,   Des - cend to__ us,__ we pray;
4. O   ho - ly Child of   Beth - le - hem,   Des - cend to__ us,   we pray;

A.1
A.2
O   ho - ly Child,

(with 8ves ad lib.)

30. O COME, O COME, EMMANUEL

(Veni, veni, Emmanuel)

Words 18th century
tr. T. A. LACEY

Melody from 15th-century
French Franciscan Processional★
adapted and arranged by
DAVID WILLCOCKS

1. O come, O come, Em-ma-nu-el! Re-deem thy cap-tive Is-ra-el, That in-to ex-ile drear is gone Far from the face of God's dear Son.
5. O come, O come, A-do-na-ï, Who in thy glo-rious ma-jes-ty From that high moun-tain clothed with awe Gav-est thy folk the el-der law.

REFRAIN

Em-ma-nu-el Shall come to thee,

Re-joice! Re-joice! Em-ma-nu-el Shall come to thee, O Is-ra-el.

★Paris, Bib. Nat. Fonds Latin MS. 10581
Congregation/Audience should sing sections marked ⌐ ¬ of verses 1, 2, 4 and 5.
† This hymn may be sung unaccompanied.
Words from *The English Hymnal* by permission of Oxford University Press.

VERSES 2 and 4

A.1

mf 2. O come, thou Branch of Jes - se! draw The quar-ry from the li - on's claw; From
mf 4. O come, thou Lord of Da - vid's Key! The roy-al door fling wide and free; Safe-

S.1 / S.2 (or piano)

*Ah*_____ *Ah*_____ *Ah*_

A.2

Ah *Ah* *Ah*

the dread ca-verns of _____ the grave, From ne-ther hell, thy peo - ple save.
-guard for us the heav'n-ward road, And bar the way to death's _ a - bode.

*Ah*_____ (piano)

*Ah*_____

REFRAIN

after v. 2: straight on for v. 3
after v. 4: D.C. for v. 5

A.1 *f*

Re-joice! Re-joice! Em - ma - nu-el Shall come to thee, O Is - ra - el.

S.1 / S.2 *f*

Re-joice! Re-joice! Em - ma - nu-el_ Shall come_to_thee, O_ Is - ra - el.

A.2 *f*

PIANO *f*

after v. 2: straight on for v. 3
after v. 4: D.C. for v. 5

VERSE 3

A.1

mp

3. O come, O come, thou Day - spring bright!   Pour on our souls thy heal - ing light; Dis-

S.1
S.2
(or
piano)

pp

Come,   thou   Day-spring bright! Pour on our souls   thy   heal - ing light; Dis -

A.2

pp

- pel the long night's lin - g'ring gloom, And pierce the sha-dows of ____ the tomb.   *Re-*

cresc.

REFRAIN

f

- pel the long night's lin - g'ring gloom, And ___ pierce the sha-dows of   the   tomb. *Re -*

cresc.

f (piano)

cresc.

f (piano)

Back to p.120 for v.4

- joice!   Re-joice!   Em - ma - nu-el Shall come to thee, O Is - ra - el.

- joice!   Re-joice!   Em - ma - nu - el Shall come to thee, O Is - ra - el.

Back to p.120 for v.4

(Piano)

31. ONCE IN ROYAL DAVID'S CITY

(unaccompanied version)

Words by
C. F. ALEXANDER

H. J. GAUNTLETT
arranged by DAVID WILLCOCKS

1. Once in roy-al Da-vid's ci-ty Stood a low-ly cat-tle shed,
Where a mo-ther laid her ba-by In a man-ger for his bed:

2. He came down to earth from hea-ven, Who is God and Lord of all,
And his shel-ter was a sta-ble, And his cra-dle was a stall;

Ma-ry was that mo-ther mild, Je-sus Christ her lit-tle child.
With the poor, and mean, and low-ly, Lived on earth our Sa-viour ho-ly.

3. And through all his wondrous childhood
   He would honour and obey,
   Love, and watch the lowly maiden,
   In whose gentle arms he lay;
   Christian children all must be
   Mild, obedient, good as he.

4. For he is our childhood's pattern,
   Day by day like us he grew,
   He was little, weak, and helpless,
   Tears and smiles like us he knew;
   And he feeleth for our sadness,
   And he shareth in our gladness.

5. And our eyes at last shall see him,
   Through his own redeeming love,
   For that child so dear and gentle
   Is our Lord in heaven above;
   And he leads his children on
   To the place where he is gone.

6. Not in that poor low - ly____ sta - ble,

With____ the ox - en stand - ing____ by,

We shall see him; but____ in____ hea - ven,

Set at God's right hand____ on____ high;

Where____ like stars his child - ren crowned____

wait a - round.

All____ in____ white shall____ wait____ a - round.

31a. ONCE IN ROYAL DAVID'S CITY

(congregational version)

Words by
C. F. ALEXANDER

H. J. GAUNTLETT
arranged by DAVID WILLCOCKS

♩ = 63

1. Once in roy - al Da - vid's ci - ty Stood a low - ly cat - tle— shed,
Where a mo - ther laid— her— ba - by In a man - ger for— his— bed:

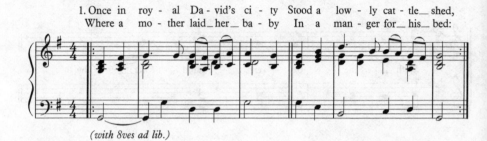

(with 8ves ad lib.)

Ma - ry was that mo - ther mild, Je - sus Christ her lit - tle— child.

2. He came down to earth from heaven,
 Who is God and Lord of all,
And his shelter was a stable,
 And his cradle was a stall;
With the poor, and mean, and lowly
Lived on earth our Saviour holy.

3. And through all his wondrous childhood
 He would honour and obey,
Love, and watch the lowly maiden,
 In whose gentle arms he lay;
Christian children all must be‿
Mild, obedient, good as he.

4. For he is our childhood's pattern,
 Day by day like us he grew,
He was little, weak, and helpless,
 Tears and smiles like us he knew;
And he feeleth for our sadness,
And he shareth in our gladness.

5. And our eyes at last shall see him,
 Through his own redeeming love,
For that child so dear and gentle
 Is our Lord in heaven above;
And he leads his children on
To the place where he is gone.

Homage to R.V.W.

32. SUSSEX CAROL

English traditional carol
arranged by DAVID WILLCOCKS

Melody and words reprinted by permission of Ursula Vaughan Williams

1st time (v. 1)

SOPRANOS

an - gels bring— News   of   great joy,_ news of__ great mirth,
made   us glad,

FULL

News   of   our   mer - ci - ful__ King's birth.

2nd time (v. 2)

SOPRANOS

When from our sin__ he set__ us free,____   All   for   to__

ALTOS

(voices unaccompanied)

128   Sussex carol

All for to see the new - born King.

All____ for____ to____ see the new - born King.

(8va)

S.1
S.2
S.3★

A.
(or A.1★)

Ah_____

4. All out of dark – ness we__ have light, Which

legato

1st time   2nd time

made the an – gels sing this night: All sing this night:

1st time   2nd time

★S.3 may be sung by 2nd altos if preferred.

33. PERSONENT HODIE

Words from *Piae Cantiones*, 1582

German melody, 1360
arranged by JOHN RUTTER

from *Dancing Day*, a cycle of traditional carols arranged by John Rutter

vir-,   vir-,   Et de vir – gi – ne – o   ven-tre pro-cre – a – tus.

SOPRANOS

2. In mun-do

na – sci – tur,   Pan-nis in – vol – vi – tur,   Prae-se – pi   po – ni – tur

Sta-bu – lo bru – to – rum,   Rec-tor su-per – no – rum,   Per-di – dit,

D♭

34. PAST THREE A CLOCK

Words by
G. R. WOODWARD
(Words of refrain
traditional)

English traditional carol
arranged by
JOHN RUTTER

Lyrics from music:

SOPRANO: Past three a clock, And a cold frosty morning:

ALTO: Past three a clock; Good morrow, masters all!

VERSES 1, 3, 5, 7

1. Born is a baby, Gentle as may be, Son of th'eternal Father supernal.
3. Mid earth rejoices Hearing such voices Ne'er to-fore so well Caroling Nowell.
5. Cheese from the dairy Bring they for Mary, And, not for money, Butter and honey.
7. Myrrh from full coffer, Incense they offer: Nor is the golden Nugget withholden.

Words reprinted from *The Cambridge Carol Book* by permission of The Society for Promoting Christian Knowledge

Past three a clock, And a cold frosty morn-ing:

Past three a clock; Good morrow, mas-ters all!

VERSES 2, 4, 6, 8

S. 1

2. Se-raph quire sing - eth, An - gel bell
4. Hinds o'er the pearl - y Dew - y
6. Light out of star - land Lead -
8. Thus they: I pray you, Up, sirs, nor

S. 2

2. Se-raph quire sing - eth, An - gel bell ring-eth:
4. Hinds o'er the pearl - y Dew-y lawn ear - ly
6. Light out of star - land Lead-eth from far land
8. Thus they: I pray you, Up, sirs, nor stay you

A.

2. Se-raph quire sing - eth, An - gel bell
4. Hinds o'er the pearl - y Dew - y
6. Light out of star - land Lead -
8. Thus they: I pray you, Up, sirs, nor

rings. Hark___ how they time it, and_ chime it.
lawn Seek___ the high stran-ger in the man-ger.
-eth Prin - ces, to Wor-ship and_ greet him.
stay Till___ ye con-fess him and_ bless him.

Hark how_ they_ rime it, Time it, and chime it.
Seek the_ high_ stran - ger Laid in the man-ger.
Prin - ces,_ to __ meet him, Wor-ship and greet him.
Till_ ye_ con - fess him Like-wise, and bless him.

rings. Hark_ how_ they time it, and_ chime it.
lawn Seek_ the _ high stran - ger in the man-ger.
-eth Prin - ces_ to Wor - ship and_ greet him.
stay Till_ ye_ con - fess him and_ bless him.

REFRAIN (after vv. 2, 4, 6, 8)

Past three a clock, And a cold_ fro-sty

Past three a clock, And a cold_ fro-sty morn - ing:

Past three a clock, And a cold_ fro-sty

after Verses 2, 4, 6: D.%
after Verse 8: Fine

morn - ing: Past three a clock; Good mor-row, mas-ters all!

Past three a clock; Good mor-row, mas-ters all!___

morn - ing: Past three a clock; Good mor-row, mas-ters_ all!

35. QUEM PASTORES LAUDAVERE

(Shepherds left their flocks a-straying)

Words tr.
IMOGEN HOLST

German, 14th century
arranged by JOHN RUTTER

English words reprinted by permission of G. & I. Holst Ltd.

SOPRANO SOLO or SEMI-CHORUS

mf dolce

3. Chri - sto re - gi, De - o na - to, Per___ Ma - ri - am
3. *Let   us   now   in   ev - 'ry   na - tion   Sing___ his   praise___ with*

mp

S.

Hum (or sing *Ah*)

mp

A.

cresc.

no - bis da - to, Me - ri - to   re - so - net ve - re
ex - ul - ta - tion.   All   the world   shall   find   sal - va - tion

cresc.

cresc.

f dolce   *p*

Laus, ho - nor___ et glo - ri - a,   Laus, ho - nor___ et glo - ri - a.
In   the birth___ of   Ma - ry's Son,   In   the birth___ of   Ma - ry's Son.

mf   *p*

mf   *p*

36. QUELLE EST CETTE ODEUR AGRÉABLE?

(Whence is that goodly fragrance flowing?)

Tr. A. B. RAMSAY
(v. 4 tr. DAVID WILLCOCKS)

French traditional carol
arranged by DAVID WILLCOCKS

★Accompanying voices in this carol may hum or sing *Ah*, if preferred.

English words of vv. 1—3 reprinted by permission of the Master and Fellows of Magdalene College, Cambridge

S.1 ★
2. Mais quelle é - cla - tan - te lu - miè - - - re Dans la nuit vient frap-per nos yeux!
2. What is that light so bril - liant, break - - - ing Here in the night a - cross our eyes?

S.2 ★
2. Mais quelle é - cla - tan - te lu - miè - - re Dans_ la nuit_ vient frap-per nos yeux!
2. What is that light so bril - liant, break - - ing Here_ in the_ night a - cross our eyes?

A.
2. Mais quelle é - cla - tan - te lu - miè - re Dans la nuit vient frap - per nos yeux!
2. What is that light so bril - liant, break - ing Here in the night a - cross our eyes?

L'as - tre du jour, dans sa___ car - riè - re,
Nev - er so bright, the day - star___ wak - ing,

L'as - tre du jour, dans sa___ car - riè - re,
Nev - er so bright, the day - star wak - ing,

L'as - tre du jour, dans sa car - riè - re,
Nev - er so bright, the day - star wak - ing,

★Verse 2 should be sung by a few sopranos only, with all altos; sopranos may sing *Ah*.

Fût - il   ja - mais   si ra - dieux?
Start - ed   to   climb   the morn-ing skies!

Fût - il   ja - mais   si   ra - - - dieux?
Start - ed   to   climb   the   morn - - ing   skies!

Fût - il   ja - mais   si   ra - - - dieux?
Start - ed   to   climb   the   morn - - ing   skies!

Mais quelle é - cla - tan - te   lu - miè - -
What   is   that   light so bril - liant,   break - -

Mais quelle é - cla - tan - te_____ lu - miè -
What   is   that   light   so   bril - - liant,   break - -

Mais quelle é - cla - tan - te   lu - miè - re
What   is   that   light   so   bril - - liant, break - ing

- - re Dans   la   nuit   vient frap-per   nos yeux!
- - ing Here   in   the   night a-cross   our eyes?

- - re Dans__ la   nuit__ vient frap-per   nos   yeux!
- - ing Here__ in   the__   night a-cross   our   eyes?

Dans   la   nuit   vient   frap - per   nos   yeux!
Here   in   the   night   a - cross   our   eyes?

S.1

p

3. A Beth - lé - em,   dans u - ne crè - che,
3. Beth - le - hem! there   in   man - ger   ly - ing,

S.2

pp

3. A Beth - lé - em,   dans u - ne____ crè - che,
3. Beth - le - hem! there   in   man - ger____ ly - ing,

A.

pp

3. A Beth - lé - em, dans u - ne crè - che, Il____
3. Beth - le - hem! there in man - ger ly - ing, Find____

Il vient de vous naî - tre un Sau - veur;
Find your Re - deem - er,   haste a - - way,

Il vient de____ vous naî - - tre un Sau - veur;
Find your Re - deem - er,____   haste a - way,

____ vient de vous naî - tre un____ Sau - veur;
____ your Re - deem - er,   haste____ a - - way,

cresc.

Al - lons, que rien ne vous em - pê - che
Run ye with ea - ger foot - steps hie - ing!

cresc.

Al - lons, que rien ne vous em - pê - che, que rien ne vous em - pê - che
Run ye with ea - ger foot-steps hie - ing, with ea - ger foot-steps hie - ing!

cresc.

Al - lons,   que rien ne vous____ em - pê - che____
Run ye   with ea - ger foot - steps hie - ing!

f *ma dolce*

S.1
4. Dieu tout-puis - sant,   gloire é - ter - nel - le
4. *Praise to the Lord of all cre - a - tion,*

S.2
4. Dieu tout-puis - sant,__ gloire é-ter-nel - le
4. *Praise to the Lord__ of all cre-a - tion,*

A.1
4. Dieu tout-puis - sant,__ gloire é - ter-nel - le
4. *Praise to the Lord__ of all cre - a - tion,*

A.2
4. Dieu tout-puis - sant,   gloire é - ter-nel - le__
4. *Praise to the Lord of all cre-a - tion,__*

Vous soit ren - du - e jus - qu'aux cieux;
Glo - ry to God, the fount of grace;

Vous soit ren - du - e jus - qu'aux cieux;
Glo - ry to__ God, the fount of grace;

Vous__ soit ren - du - e__ jus - qu'aux cieux;
Glo - ry to__ God, the fount of grace;

__ Vous soit ren - du - e jus - - qu'aux cieux;
Glo - ry to God, the fount__ of grace;

Que la paix soit u - ni - ver - sel - le,
May peace a - bide in ev - 'ry na - tion,

Que la paix soit u - ni - ver - sel - le,
May peace a - bide in ev - 'ry__ na - tion,

Que la paix soit u - ni - ver - sel - le,
May peace a - bide in ev - 'ry__ na - tion,

Que la paix soit u - ni - ver - sel - le,
May peace a - bide in ev - 'ry na - tion,

37. SEE AMID THE WINTER'S SNOW

Words by
E. CASWALL

JOHN GOSS
arranged by DAVID WILLCOCKS

† This carol may be sung unaccompanied.

CHORUS

(with 8ves ad lib.)

Hail, thou ev - er - bless - ed morn;   Hail, re-demp-tion's hap-py dawn;

Sing through all Je - ru - sa - lem, ___ Christ is born in Beth-le - hem.

Ah ___   Ah ___

2. Lo, with-in a man - ger lies   He who built the star - ry skies;
5. Sa - cred in-fant, all di - vine,   What a ten - der love was thine,

Ah ___   Ah ___

*plus audience or additional voices ad lib.

152   See amid the winter's snow

S. 1 / S. 2 — *Ah_____ Ah_____*

A. 1 — *Ah_____ Ah_____*
He who, throned in height sub-lime, Sits a-mid the che-ru-bim:
Thus to come from high - est bliss Down to such a world as this:

A. 2 — *Ah_____ Ah_____*

mf cresc. ... *f cresc.* ... Sing_ *ff*
Hail, thou ev - er - bless - ed morn; Hail, re - demp-tion's hap-py_ dawn;

mf cresc. ... *f cresc.*
Hail, thou ev - er - bless - ed morn; Hail, re-demp-tion's hap-py dawn;

mf cresc. ... *f cresc.*
Hail, thou ev - er - bless - ed morn; Hail, re-demp-tion's hap-py_ dawn;

mf cresc. ... *f cresc.* ... *ff*

(with 8ves ad lib.)

after verse 5: to page 155 for last verse

ff
Sing_ through all_ Je - ru - sa - lem, Christ_____ is born_ in Beth-le - hem.

ff
Sing through all Je - ru - sa - lem, Christ is born in Beth - le - hem.

ff
Sing through all Je - ru - sa - lem,_ Christ is born in Beth - le - hem.

SOPRANOS

3. Say, ye ho - ly shep - herds, say

ALTO 1
ALTO 2

3. Say, ye ho - ly shep - herds, say___

What your joy - ful news to - day; Where - fore have ye

What_ your_ joy - ful_ news to - day; Where - fore have ye

left your sheep On the lone - ly moun - tain steep?

left your sheep On the lone - - - ly moun - tain steep?

CHORUS

S.1
S.2

Hail, thou ev - er - bless - ed_ morn; Hail, re-demp-tion's hap- py_ dawn;

A.1
A.2

(with 8ves ad lib.)

Sing through all Je - ru - sa - lem,__ Christ is born in Beth-le - hem.

'As   we watch'd at dead of night,   Lo, we   saw a

pp   *cresc.*

'As   we watch'd at dead of night,   Lo,   we

p   *cresc.*

4. 'As we watch'd at dead of night, Lo, we saw a won - drous light;

won - drous light;   An - gels sing-ing, Told us of the Sa - viour's birth:'

mf *cresc.*

mf *cresc.*

saw   a won-drous light;__ An - gels sing-ing of the Sa-viour's birth:'

f

An - gels sing - ing "Peace on earth" Told us of the Sa - viour's birth:'

CHORUS

f

ff Hail, thou ev - er - bless - ed__ morn;   Hail, re-demp-tion's__ hap - py__ dawn;

f

f

(with 8ves ad lib.)

Back to 𝄋 (p. 151) for verse 5

Sing through all Je - ru - sa - lem, Christ is born in Beth - le - hem.

6. Teach, O teach us, Ho - ly Child, By thy face so meek and mild,

Teach us to re - sem - ble thee, In thy sweet hu - mi - li - ty:

38. THE INFANT KING

Words by
S. BARING-GOULD

Basque Noël
arranged by
JOHN RUTTER

3. *Sing lullaby!*
Lullaby baby, now a-dozing,
Sing lullaby!
Hush, do not wake the Infant King.
Soon comes the cross, the nails, the piercing,
Then in the grave at last reposing:
Sing lullaby!

4. *Sing lullaby!*
Lullaby! is the babe a-waking?
Sing lullaby!
Hush, do not stir the Infant King.
Dreaming of Easter, gladsome morning,
Conquering Death, its bondage breaking:
Sing lullaby!

39. STAR CAROL

Words and music by
JOHN RUTTER
arranged by
KENNETH PONT

1. Sing this night, for a boy is born in Beth-le-hem,
2. An - gels bright, come from hea-ven's high-est glo - ry,

Christ our Lord in a low-ly man-ger lies;
Bear the news with its mes-sage of good cheer:

Bring your gifts, come and
"Sing, re - joice, for a

The original version of this carol, for mixed voices, optional children's chorus, and piano, is on sale (X 233).

wor-ship at his cra - dle, Hur-ry to Beth - le - hem__ and see the son__ of
King is come to save__ us, Hur-ry to Beth - le - hem__ and see the son__ of

Ma - ry!   See his star
Ma - ry!"

shin - ing bright In the sky this__ Christ - mas Night!

Fol - low me joy - ful - ly; Hur - ry to Beth - le - hem__

D.C. (p. 158)

1st time

2nd time

___ and see the son ___ of Ma ― ry! Ma ― ry!

p dolce e legato

3. See, he lies in his

dolce e legato

mo - ther's ten-der keep - ing; Je - sus Christ in her lov-ing arms a-sleep.

Shep - herds poor, come to wor-ship and a - dore ___ him, Of - fer their hum - ble gifts ___

be-fore the son of Ma - ry.

p legato
See his star shin - ing bright In the sky this

Christ - mas Night! Fol - low me joy - ful - ly;

Hur-ry to Beth - le - hem and see the son of Ma - ry!

4. Let us all pay our hom-age at the man - ger, Sing his praise on this joy-ful Christ-mas Night; Christ is come, bring-ing pro-mise of sal - va - tion; Hur-ry to Beth - le - hem ___ and see the son__ of Ma - ry!

Lower voice optional

See his star shin-ing bright In the sky this

Christ - mas Night! Fol - low me joy - ful - ly;

Hur-ry to Beth - le-hem and see the son of Ma - ry,

Poco largamente   cresc.   **rall.**

Hur-ry to Beth - le-hem and see the son of Ma - ry!

40. STILLE NACHT

(Silent night)

Words by
JOSEPH MOHR

FRANZ GRÜBER
arranged by
JOHN RUTTER

dim.

Aw

dim.

Ruh, _____
da, _____
- burt, _____

Schlaf'_ in himm - lisch-er　Ruh! _____
Christ,_ der Ret - ter, ist　da! _____
Christ,_ in　dei - ner Ge - burt! _____

dim.

1. Silent night, holy night,
   All is calm, all is bright
   'Round yon virgin mother and child,
   Holy infant so tender and mild,
   Sleep in heavenly peace,
   Sleep in heavenly peace.

2. Silent night, holy night,
   Shepherds first saw the sight:
   Glories stream from heaven afar,
   Heav'nly hosts sing Alleluia!
   Christ the Saviour is born,
   Christ the Saviour is born.

3. Silent night, holy night,
   Son of God, love's pure light;
   Radiance beams from thy holy face,
   With the dawn of redeeming grace,
   Jesus, Lord, at thy birth,
   Jesus, Lord, at thy birth.
                    (English words anon.)

41. LUTE-BOOK LULLABY

Words by
W. BALLET

W. BALLET (17th c.)
arranged by
JOHN RUTTER

SOPRANO

ALTO

1. Sweet was the song the Vir - gin sang,

When

When she to Beth - lem Ju - da came And

Ju - - da came

she to Beth - lem Ju - - - da came

was de - liv - ered of _ a _ son, That bless - ed

That

Je - sus hath to name: 'Lul - la, lul - la,

Je - sus

lul - la, lul - la-by.

lul - la, lul - la - by, _ Lul - la, lul - la, lul - la, lul - la - by.' 2. 'Sweet

42. THE FIRST NOWELL

English traditional carol
arranged by DAVID WILLCOCKS

1. The first Nowell the angel did say Was to

cer-tain poor shep-herds in fields as they lay; In fields where

they lay keep-ing their sheep, On a cold win-ter's night that

*This carol may be sung unaccompanied.

★Verses 2 & 4 and/or 3 & 5 may be sung unaccompanied.

gave____great light, And____ so it con - tin - ued both day____ and____ night:
stop____ and stay Right____ ov - er the place____where Je - sus____ lay:

REFRAIN

S.1
S.2

No - well,
No - well,____ No - well,____ No - well,____ No - well,

Born____

A.1
A.2

Born____

PIANO
ad lib.

Born

Born   is   the   King____   of   Is - ra - el!

The first Nowell

★Verses 2 & 4 and/or 3 & 5 may be sung unaccompanied.

43. THE HOLLY AND THE IVY

English traditional carol
arranged by
JOHN RUTTER

*This setting may be sung unaccompanied.

crown.
-viour.
all.

O ____ the ris-ing of ___ the __ sun ___ And the

The __ play-ing of the mer-ry

run-ning of ___ the deer, ___ The __

to next page for vv. 3 and 4

or - gan, Sweet __ sing-ing in the choir.

play-ing of the or-gan, sing - ing in the choir.

VERSES 3 and 4
(soli or full)

Ah

(solo or full)

3. The hol-ly bears a ber-ry   As red as a - ny blood;   And
4. The hol-ly bears a pric-kle   As sharp as a - ny thorn;   And

Ah
O   the

Ma-ry bore sweet Je-sus Christ To___ do poor sin - ners_ good.
Ma-ry bore sweet Je-sus Christ On___ Christ-mas Day in the morn.

O   the ris-ing of the___ sun,   And the
ris-ing of the   sun___   And the run - ning, And the run-ning of___ the
And the run-ning of   the   deer,   The___

after v.3: repeat this page
after v.4: back to p.174

deer,   the   or - gan, Sweet sing - ing in the choir.
play-ing of the mer-ry   or - gan, Sweet_ sing-ing in the   choir.

for the staff and pupils of Huyton College

44. GABRIEL'S MESSAGE

Words by
S. BARING-GOULD

Basque carol
arranged by
JOHN RUTTER

la - dy, Glo - - - ri - a! _____ 2. 'For

known a bless - ed Mo – ther thou shalt be, _____ All
(3.) gen – tle Ma – ry meek – ly bowed her head, _____ 'To
(2.) Aw _____ Aw
(3.) Hum
(2.) Aw
(3.) Hum
(2.) Aw _____
(3.)-a! Hum

ge – ne - ra – tions laud and hon – - our thee, _____ Thy
me be as it pleas - eth God,' _____ she said, _____ 'My
Aw _____
Aw _____

her, Em-ma-nu-el, the Christ,__ was__ born__ In __

Beth-le-hem,__ all on a Christ — mas morn, And Christ —

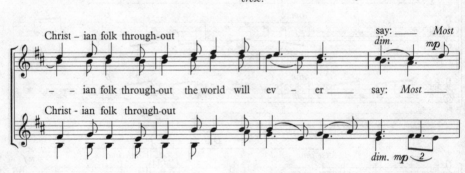

Christ — mas__ morn,__ And

— — ian folk through-out the world will ev — er __ say: Most __

high-ly fa-voured la — dy,__ Glo — — — ri — a!

45. THERE IS NO ROSE

Words: 15th century

BENJAMIN BRITTEN

was Hea-ven and earth in li-tel space,   Res mi - ran - da,___

___ Res mi - ran - da.   By that rose we   may well see

There be one God   in   per-sons three,   Pa-res for - ma,___   pa-res

46. THE LINDEN TREE CAROL

Words tr.
G. R. WOODWARD

German traditional carol
arranged by
JOHN RUTTER

Andante con moto
VERSES 1, 2 and 5

1. There stood___ in heav'n___ a lin - den tree, But, though___ 'twas___ ho - ney-la - - - den, All an - gels cried, 'No bloom___ shall be___ Like that___ of___ one___ fair maid - - - en.'

2. Sped Ga - bri - el___ on wing - èd feet, And passed___ through bolt - ed por - - - tals, In Na - za - reth, a maid___ to greet,___ Blest o'er___ all___ o - ther mor - - - tals.

5. This ti - ding fill'd___ his mates___ with glee: 'Twas passed___ from one___ to o - - - ther, That 'twas___ Ma - ry, and none___ but she,___ And God___ would call___ her Mo - - - ther.

'No___
a___
and___

VERSES 3 and 4
v. 3: 1st SOLO VOICE
v. 4: 2nd SOLO VOICE

3. 'Hail Ma — ry!' quoth the an — gel mild, 'Of
4. 'So be it!' God's hand — mai — den cried, 'Ac —

S.

CHOIR

3. *Ah*
4. *Hum*

A.

wo — man — kind the fair — — est: The
-cord — ing to thy tell — — ing.' Where-

Vir — gin ay shalt thou be styled, A
-on the an — gel smart — ly hied Up

after v.3: repeat this page
after v.4: D.C. for v.5

babe al — though thou bear — — — est.'
home — ward to his dwell — — — ing.

47. TOMORROW SHALL BE MY DANCING DAY

English traditional carol
arranged by JOHN RUTTER

SOLO SOPRANO (or SEMI-CHORUS)

1. To-mor-row shall be__ my danc-ing day: I would__ my

true__ love did__ so chance To__ see the le-gend of__ my

play, To call my true__ love to__ my dance: *Sing O my__*

from *Dancing Day*, a cycle of traditional carols arranged by John Rutter

love, O my love, my love, my love; This have I done for my true love. To-mor-row shall be my danc-ing day: I would my true love did so chance To see the le-gend of my play, To call my true love to my

dance: Sing O my_ love, O_ my love, my

love, my love; This have I done_ for my_ true love.

S.1 2. Then was_ I

S.2 2. Then_

day: I would my true love did so chance To

see the le - gend of my play, To call my

E   *ff*

1 true love to my dance. Sing O my

2 true love to my dance. Sing O my love,

dim.   *mf*   *f cresc.*

love, O my love, my love; This

dim.   *mf*   *f cresc.*

O my love, my love, my love; This have I

48. UNTO US IS BORN A SON

Words tr.
G. R. WOODWARD

Tune from *Piae Cantiones*, 1582
arranged by DAVID WILLCOCKS

1. Un - to us is born a Son, King of quires su - per - nal:

(with 8ves ad lib.)

See on earth his life be - gun, Of lords the Lord e -

Words reprinted from *The Cowley Carol Book* by permission of A. R. Mowbray & Co. Ltd.

CHOIR UNACCOMPANIED★

SOPRANO

2. Christ, from heav'n des - cend - ing low, ___ Comes on ___ earth ___ a

ALTO

stran - ger; Ox and ass their own - er ___ know, Be - cra - dled in the

man - ger, be - cra - dled in the ___ man - ger.

★May be sung accompanied, or by unison voices and piano as in verse 1.

CHOIR and CONGREGATION

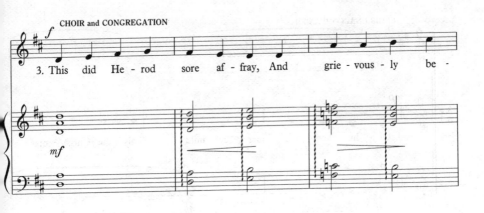

3. This did He - rod sore af - fray, And grie - vous - ly be -

- wil - der, So he gave the word to slay, And

slew the lit - tle chil - der, and slew the lit - tle chil - der.

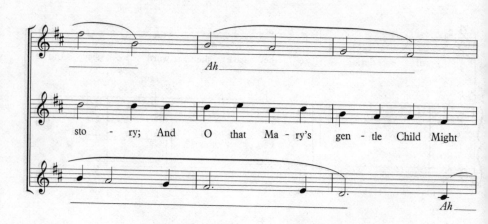

*Congregation sings melody (1st alto part).

for Llywela Harris and the Choir of Abbots Bromley School

49. A MERRY CHRISTMAS

English traditional carol
arranged by
JOHN RUTTER

pud – ding   And   bring   some   out   here.   Good   tid – ings — we —

bring   us some fig – gy   pud – ding   out   here.   Good   tid – ings   we

bring — To   you   and   your   kin;   We   wish   you   a   mer – ry

bring   To   you   and   your   kin;   We   wish   you   a   mer – ry

Christ – mas And a   hap – py — New   Year. —   For   we   all   like — fig – gy

Christ – mas And a   hap – py   New   Year.   Ah ——————————

pud – ding,   Ah ——————————————   For we   all   like — fig – gy

—   For we   all   like — fig – gy pud – ding, For we   all   like   fig – gy

pud – ding,   So   bring   some   out   here.   Good

pud – ding,   So   bring   some   out   here. —   Good   tid – ings   we

204 A merry Christmas

50. WHILE SHEPHERDS WATCHED THEIR FLOCKS

Words by
NAHUM TATE (1652–1715)

Este's Psalter, 1592
arranged by DAVID WILLCOCKS

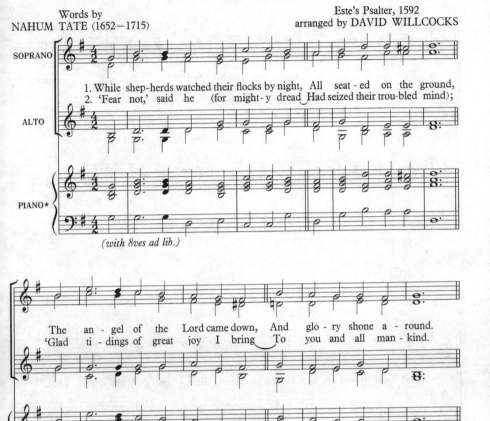

1. While shep-herds watched their flocks by night, All seat-ed on the ground,
2. 'Fear not,' said he (for might-y dread Had seized their trou-bled mind);

The an-gel of the Lord came down, And glo-ry shone a-round.
'Glad ti-dings of great joy I bring To you and all man-kind.

(with 8ves ad lib.)

3. 'To you in David's town this day
   Is born of David's line
   A Saviour, who is Christ the Lord;
   And this shall be the sign:

4. 'The heavenly Babe you there shall find
   To human view displayed,
   All meanly wrapped in swathing bands,
   And in a manger laid.'

5. Thus spake the Seraph; and forthwith
   Appeared a shining throng
   Of angels praising God, who thus
   Addressed their joyful song:

6. 'All glory be to God on high,
   And on the earth be peace;
   Good-will henceforth from heaven to men
   Begin and never cease.'

*(to next page for alternative
version of v.6)*

★This hymn may be sung unaccompanied in A major.

Alternative version for Verse 6

6. 'All glo - ry be to God on high, And on the earth be peace;

(with 8ves ad lib.)

Good - will hence-forth from heaven to men Be - gin and nev - er cease.'

Processed and printed by
Halstan & Co. Ltd., Amersham, Bucks., England

THE NINE LESSONS

❡ *The Congregation, standing, shall be bidden to prayer in these words:*

BELOVED in Christ, at this Christmas-tide let it be our care and delight to hear again the message of the angels, and in heart and mind to go even unto Bethlehem and see this thing which is come to pass, and the Babe lying in a manger.

Therefore let us read and mark in Holy Scripture the tale of the loving purposes of God from the first days of our disobedience unto the glorious Redemption brought us by this Holy Child.

But first, let us pray for the needs of the whole world; for peace on earth and goodwill among all his people; for unity and brotherhood within the Church he came to build, and especially in this our diocese.

And because this would rejoice his heart, let us remember, in his name, the poor and helpless, the cold, the hungry, and the oppressed; the sick and them that mourn, the lonely and the unloved, the aged and the little children; all those who know not the Lord Jesus, or who love him not, or who by sin have grieved his heart of love.

Lastly, let us remember before God all those who rejoice with us, but upon another shore, and in a greater light, that multitude which no man can number, whose hope was in the Word made flesh, and with whom in the Lord Jesus we are one for evermore.

These prayers and praises let us humbly offer up to the Throne of Heaven, in the words which Christ himself hath taught us:

OUR Father, which art in heaven, Hallowed be thy name; Thy kingdom come; Thy will be done; In earth as it is in heaven. Give us this day our daily bread. And forgive us our trespasses, As we forgive them that trespass against us. And lead us not into temptation; But deliver us from evil: For thine is the kingdom, The power, and the glory, For ever and ever. Amen.

❡ *Then shall the Congregation sit.*
[The Readers of the Lessons should be appointed after a definite order; in a Cathedral, for instance, from a Chorister up to a Bishop.
Each Reader should proceed to the Reading Desk at the beginning of the last verse of the preceding carol; and announce his Lesson by the descriptive sentence attached to it. At the end of the Lesson, the Reader should pause and say: Thanks be to God.]

FIRST LESSON
God announces in the Garden of Eden that the seed of woman shall bruise the serpent's head. GENESIS III, 8–15

SECOND LESSON
God promises to faithful Abraham that in his seed shall the nations of the earth be blessed. GENESIS XXII, 15–18

THIRD LESSON
Christ's birth and kingdom are foretold by Isaiah. ISAIAH IX, 2, 6, 7

FOURTH LESSON
The peace that Christ will bring is foreshown.   ISAIAH XI, 1, 2, 3a, 4a, 6–9

ALTERNATIVE FOURTH LESSON
The prophet Micah foretells the glory of little Bethlehem.   MICAH V, 2–4

FIFTH LESSON
The angel Gabriel salutes the Blessed Virgin Mary.   ST LUKE I, 26–35, 38

ALTERNATIVE FIFTH LESSON
The prophet in exile foresees the coming of the glory of the Lord.   ISAIAH LX, 1–6, 19

SIXTH LESSON
St Matthew tells of the birth of Jesus.   ST MATTHEW I, 18–23

ALTERNATIVE SIXTH LESSON
St Luke tells of the birth of Jesus.   ST LUKE II, 1, 3–7

SEVENTH LESSON
The shepherds go to the manger.   ST LUKE II, 8–16

EIGHTH LESSON
The wise men are led by the star to Jesus.   ST MATTHEW II, 1–11

¶   *The Congregation shall stand for the ninth lesson.*

NINTH LESSON
St John unfolds the great mystery of the Incarnation.   ST JOHN I, 1–14

Priest The Lord be with you.
Answer And with thy spirit.
Priest Let us pray.

¶   *All kneel.*

THE COLLECT FOR CHRISTMAS EVE
O GOD, who makest us glad with the yearly remembrance of the birth of thy only Son, Jesus Christ: Grant that as we joyfully receive him for our redeemer, so we may with sure confidence behold him, when he shall come to be our judge; who liveth and reigneth with thee and the Holy Ghost, one God, world without end. *Amen.*

Or,

THE COLLECT FOR CHRISTMAS DAY
ALMIGHTY GOD, who hast given us thy only-begotten Son to take our nature upon him, and as at this time to be born of a pure Virgin: Grant that we being regenerate, and made thy children by adoption and grace, may daily be renewed by thy Holy Spirit; through the same our Lord Jesus Christ, who liveth and reigneth with thee and the same Spirit, ever one God, world without end. *Amen.*

THE BLESSING
MAY he who by his Incarnation gathered into one things earthly and heavenly, fill you with the sweetness of inward peace and goodwill; and the blessing of God Almighty, the Father, the Son, and the Holy Ghost, be upon you and remain with you always. *Amen.*